First Printing, 2017

ISBN-10: 1546725504

ISBN-13: 978-1546725503

WE ARE LEGION

Goal for this book:

A Sinner to accept Jesus Christ as their personal Lord and Savior

Contents

SONNET

Who Wrote This?

Gracious LORD use this poem for your glory

He's healing the sick to make the deaf hear

Your resurrection gave us new stories

Beginning of wisdom, the LORD we fear

We've dismantled everything you built up

Ignorantly destroying self-temple

It is written, "[1]Knowledge puffeth up"

Assignment abandoned, life's popped pimple

As we cry "Jesus, please do for me"

While we keep singing His hands are folded

Roll in self-pity to have sympathy

As these test are given, we are molded

Through this stanza LORD, my hands have been used

To stricken peoples' heart with words that bruise.

The Word: Seek

Christ I'm enquiring of your presence

Calling for help, did you get the message?

Be watchful while praying all the daylong

[2]The LORD JEHOVAH is my strength, my song.

Fall on the ground as a humble servant,

Speak the Word in season, and stay fervent.

Not a hearer be a doer, do well,

A mindset free is no longer in jail.

More than quoting scriptures with a new dance.

When everything fails, the word will stand.

Open the bible to have some quiet time,

Digest the meat of God it will be fine.

Keep the word of God hidden in thine heart,

Meditate to seek His face is a start.

Walking In My Wealthy Place

One thing I requested and desired

That I will have a tongue which speak the truth

Because I know Satan is a liar

I believe Jesus died for me and you

Christ is the Sheppard for Him, I am slain

Christians being anchored in the word

We are prosecuted in Jesus name

Rejoicing at times even when we hurt

Holy bible states, stay fervent in prayer

God never makes mistakes, sleeps nor slumber

Our God is a judge, a lawyer, who's fair

I will stand boldly also speak humble

On this day, the decision is ours

Live for Christ or die being devoured?

Anointed To Die

Holy Spirit increase as I decrease

To abide in me, not just be wordy

When the flesh is dead, my God, I will please

Christ was anointed because I'm dirty

Behold the glory, His beauty thereof

That's [3]Saint Luke chapter nine verse twenty-three

Jesus was anointed because He's love

Crucify flesh so it can D.I.E

Written in Matthew 22:14

[4]For many are called but few are chosen

The born again Christian, who is redeemed

God wants to mend every heart broken

Cameras record because I've survived

Bless my soul to be anointed to die.

Broken For Ministry

I will serve empty ready to be filled

"Yes" to the kingdom, "no" to how I feel

Anointing cost something I did not know

Attitude to gratitude ways to flow

Be done with saying this, "God know my heart"

My walls fall down as I begin to start…

Revealing broken pieces, kept hidden

Dressed up sin like I needed no fixing

Spoke about broken, my heart was shattered

First, church hurt while the enemies gathered

Kingdom agent love for ministry died

Being an usher when I want to hide

I've learned when you hear me say, "I'm broken"

Yes, I'm broken, broken for ministry

Disconnect-It

Disconnect what doesn't bring God glory

Associates and friends won't be a choice

When clouds hang low, vision become blurry

Disconnected by force, Lord, you're my source

Midnight hour when thoughts become heavy

If it don't please God, don't resurrect it

Apartment, education, the Chevy

All of those thingsw, you have disconnect it

[5]My refuge, my fortress, my God, I trust

My exceeding joy, my lamp, my strong rock

Delivered me from spirits of lusting

Bound with succubus, my stumbling block

Different seasons along with toxins

Earth to heaven, Christ the best connection

And… I Pray

[6]First Thessalonians five: seventeen

Always warring as an intercessor

And… Continue to pray without ceasing

Taken the test while God is the teacher

And… Pray because He answers the righteous

[7]No weapon formed against thee shall prosper

Wrestle not devils who fight against us

The blood still working and covering me

And… I'm praying my business will be straight

Before Christ second coming for the saints

So we can all gather at heaven's gate

Mount up together in numbers, no rank

And… I pray this has ministered to yall

To encourage yourself instead of fall

Delivered Captive

I've been chained down in bondage for so long

I wonder what is it like to be free?

Slave mentality, humming gospel songs

Currently the shackles still on my feet

A prisoner who's trying to escape

Rather have pleasure in worldly things

"I won't succeed", my mental cassette tape

But I want freedom and the joy it brings

Now it's time to change my whole thought process

 As I depend on Jehovah, my strength

No more bondage, stress, or being depressed

Giving Jesus my all, not just a tenth

Feels good being healed, delivered, set free

Thank God for saving a sinner like me.

Breathe On Me

Tear drop of water fell slow from my eyes

Motions in hope, welcoming the needy

Crown of glory on my head is the prize

Eating every word from God, greedy

Consume my life with your laboring works

Baptized in the spirit and righteousness

I'll take notes as a server, and a clerk

Lord, you can have all of me, your Highness

Fill this place with yoke destroying power

Obedience in the heart of people

Prepared a generation with favor

Crying, pleading to dwell in this temple

Burn in me Jesus, fire revival

Move of God that can't be in denial

Set Apart

I can't say "no" to His will anymore,

Me, every Sunday hitting the floor.

It's time to come from among them, stay out,

Y'all ever saw a flower grow from grout?

This is a hard narrow place to go through,

I can't keep you and expect God's love too

Despite flaws, His perfect will must be done,

Goodbye turnt times I've enjoyed the fun.

LORD, lead me on the straight and narrow path,

Add more prayer, remove the fake, now that's math.

Christ's mercies are keeping me covered,

The midnight hour, He's my soul brother.

'Be ye separate' that's what God told me,

Are you set apart, saved to be holy?

Under the Anointing

God enquires of the man who's humble,

Steady blessed with a word like a fresh wind.

Waiting for glory without a mumble,

Climbing Jacob's latter, angels descend.

Seems as if blessings over take me more,

Although long-suffering is sure to come.

Proverbs 31, a delivered whore,

Jesus use my hands to help the kingdom.

This anointing ain't happen overnight,

Many times seeking Gods very own heart.

Loving people when flesh wanted to fight,

Several ways I became set apart.

Mantles are real, something's I don't play with,

A person that's not dismayed or dismissed.

Sonnet

Gift of poetry which has been given,

Ink pens I hold tight, got my head swimming.

Grasp thoughts in the air,

Words as fire and brimstone, I swear.

Demonic forces gotta release me,

Pull strong holds down, it's a catastrophe.

Always filled the belly with unknown lust,

Lost the love and can't find any trust.

Imperfect for three years since I've been saved,

Wavering like a ship in all my ways.

Asked for help, walking in the wilderness,

It wasn't Satan, I dug my own ditch.

Gifts come without repentance,

God has to be tired of me sinning.

Another Random

Prophets' choice of sin remains in darkness,

A seer on point with discernment, sharpness.

Praying and fasting doesn't seem to help,

Bound by my sins again as Jesus wept.

Carried my cross as if it's weight was light,

This is a spiritual war that I fight.

I say Jesus is the strength of my life,

One more opportunity to get right.

So this day Jesus, I repent to you,

I'm tired of making you shame, it's true.

A title doesn't make someone perfect,

Usher souls in the Kingdom assertive.

Before another lie depart my lips,

Shut my mouth cause this is only a gift.

Repenting Sinner & Redeemed Saint

I've been standing here stuck for quite awhile

You resemble me in my younger age

Clothes are dirty and my ways are defiled

Best actress award as though we're on stage

Inquired of He whom make all things new

Stop and think twice, "Should I be acting out"

I'm the lost sheep who requires rescue

Listen to His words proceed from my mouth

Repeated daily looking at my faults

Willing for change if you want the Sheppard

Again crying, pleading as a result

Washed in His blood, no longer a leopard

Thoughtful of my eternal resting place

Lord, until you come, again help me wait.

He Knew How to Love Me

We started as strangers then became friends
Being there for each other thick and thin
Few years passed by, we were closer than close
Words smooth as butter, then I became toast
Every way deceit was within us
His actions were bold, then I fell in lust
We finished each other's lines, O M glee
Within six words, he knew how to love me
Our characteristics were adjacent
He stroked my pride whispering dirty hints
Manner of evil took me by the hand
I grasped for oxygen sinking in sand
Reality kicked in, I then realized
The devil creeped in through someone else life

Now Faith Is…

"[8]Now faith is the substance of things hoped for,

The evidence of things not seen."

Standing on the word when life is unsure,

In adulthood acting as seventeen.

Speak with authority in existence,

And a seeds faith will have a mountain removed.

Scripture [9]Luke 7:50 for instance,

Overcoming failure and love reproof.

To know each noonday fast shall manifest,

Experience with patience will take place.

Staying on alert mode during a test,

Carry God's glory toward the worlds' space.

Now faith, is believing more than enough,

First, faith in Jesus first, then follows trust.

Anointed to Give

Give, which means transfer something that is due

Also a noun, a person, place or thing

Participate willingly, contribute

A person petitioning for the KING

No hold ups, no setbacks, and no delays

Envelope full of word bestowed upon

Sowed in dry ground, take the stench smell away

Become a lender, it's not always fun

Many encouraging words handed out

Let someone have a free smile with a hug

Offer praise along with a Judah shout

Be obedient, it won't be a tug

Carnal minds don't recognize Gods glory

Jesus the only one can change stories

Treacherously Delivered

You're here, came to me repeatedly

I forgave you, because of sovereignty

You only call my name when in trouble

Serving two masters with dealing double

I've always kept you from digging in mess

I'm your comfort in your unfaithfulness

"Give me another opportunity"

Your generation is filled with deceit

Begging me to take away unclean stuff

Knowing years ago, it's a breach of trust

Jesus didn't let your mind become sick

I presented you faultless playing tricks

Through that, it was you who I considered

To not be treacherously delivered.

The Purge

We went to the throne of Grace at His feet

Waling and travailing for a ridding

No longer wanting that unclean feeling

Tired of running on self and be beat

"[10]Purge me with hyssop, and I shall be clean:

Wash me and I shall be whiter than snow"

That is a bible verse we should all know

LORD, you purify by separating

Humbleness, we should be to seek His face

Pray when it's inconvenient is a must

Stop missing the mark and shake off the dust

We need Jesus dwelling within this place

Lose our will to your spiritual release

Will the flesh die now or become the beast

To Be Honest

This time wasn't like other times before

Exposing me crying behind closed doors

Finally confessed an inner secret

Telling the Lord who's able to keep it

Stumbling over words caused by guilt, shame

Asking for guidance through heart aching pain

Trials have been giving; flesh cannot bare

Afraid of the truth, from eyes, with a stare

I want to stand strong while the war takes place

Flesh is weak in His presence, self can't stay

My mind still running but flesh runs in fear

Of the day He calls and my ears won't hear

This sonnet is for every lost sheep

Jesus Christ has groomed and allowed to speak

Walking in My Wealthy Place Pt. 2

What did you think of when I said wealthy?

I'm covered in love, peace, joy plus healthy.

This place ain't appear to me over night,

It took years of sojourning, living right.

Expensive things are good, Christ is better,

From a different cloth, no need for leather.

I lived in a home with plenty food to eat,

Spirits would visit nightly in my sleep.

The place I'm in is a "wealthy" season,

My heart keep smiling, my smile stay cheesin'.

My pockets not fat; I still trust God,

His tithes and offerings, I will not rob.

Rich in the spirit is given by grace,

This is me, walking in my wealthy place!

Set Free

An enslaved mind could not think of words,

Similar to put together, unheard.

Exterior appearance can't compare,

Bottled up emotions that shall not spare.

Open doors have been closed due to failure,

Anointing destroys the yoke, professor.

It is not a compliment without God,

Get ready for exams, sends best regards.

More than an alert everyone know,

Thank God for His glory, not just the glow.

May seem hard but keep running for your life,

Two-edged sword, the word of God cuts you right.

Not just being broken for ministry,

Broken for Jesus to heal, and, set free.

To My Husband

My apologies for letting you down,

You saw the vision when I lost my crown?

Times when I wanted to have an excuse,

Prayed to Jesus but couldn't tell the truth.

Several moments I thought about us,

Good times with each other making much fuss.

I'm honest, I let "me" get in the way,

After you gave up us, I went astray.

I asked myself, "did he see what I saw?"

There was no divorce in the court of law.

Visions of our kids going on play dates,

The dream seemed so real but I couldn't wait.

Jesus is still putting me together,

My emotions changing like the weather.

It Is Written

I've battled different spirits for years,

A pain freak to hurt, a lover of tears.

Right now I'm done from running in circles,

Blamed others while committing self-murder.

Lucifer slidered away in the dust.

My walls are down, in the rubble, there's lust.

I can now walk with my head to the sky

Jesus is the truth and Satan tells lies.

Thank you LORD for everything you've done.

Was saved by grace through your begotten Son.

Jesus Christ is the man who died for me;

Giants do die slowly in misery!

My spiritual conquest is set in stone,

My fleshy desires are dead and gone.

Continued…To My Husband

Forgive me for putting you number two
My mind made up to do your will, it's true
Help me be obedient with what's said
Bridegroom, the one who remains in my head
I use to say friend, by the words we spoke
Only helpmate by the chains you've broke
In life you've been here from the beginning
Difference from victory and winning
Since my second birth, it's you who I trust
You've ceased the talking and all of the fuss
You're not my other half instead soulmate
I want to see you in peace as I wait
I'm nothing without you, my soul you keep
Head of the household, no one can compete

So Easily Beset Us

We walked for a while, it didn't seem far

Our amour is the Word, foundation sure

Feelings of weariness also obscure

Bottled up emotions inside a jar

Where are the bombs dropping in Gilead?

Speak life into the bones considered dead

Slay demonic spirits lying in bed

We shall live without being stingy crabs

Attacked on every side and harassed

We're counted for destruction in our mind

Still not believing miracles and signs

If it's Your will, Father, let this cup pass

Distraction is real when there is no faith

It's confusion or peace which do you face?

We Are Legion

We Are Legion, we don't care for Christ return

We imitated the church all these years

Go to the alter bow down, release fear

Not acknowledging to repent, we'll burn

Self-obsession entered our hearts of Cane

Murder as we ignite spiritual wars

Lovers of pleasure, call us immoral

Don't practice what you preach, we are the same

Waited and watched as long as predicted

Others followed every step taken

Third of angels, we are the forsaken

Ruler over many, call us wicked

Heard of the abyss, we've chosen our home

Y'all aren't conquerors, We Are Legion.

HAIKU

Hear! Fret not my child

For evil doers will kill

Be not cast away

Bucked against the word

Ate the Bread and yet not filled

Children of Egypt

Disobedience

This shouldn't be from children

Obey the LORDs will

Live in the realm of

Good health and prosperity

[11]Third John One and Two

No sickness can live

Including Cancer or AIDS

Poverty must go

Take a leap of HOPE

Surpassing all negative

Confidence in Christ

Yes, prayer with fasting

Committed and submitted

Totally souled out

Strong belief in God

Not being moved by mountains

Trust without doubting

Please DO NOT look back

Peter walking on water

But this is quick sand

We walked forty years

Complained and murmured all day

Still didn't make it

Surrender to God

Sound with the voice of triumph

Victory is ours

There will be weeping

Repent, ye workers of sin

And gnashing of teeth

Shine so bright, can't see

His face only hear the voice

Proclaim the Lords fame

The glory of God

Rest upon the LORD, Jesus

We must seek His face

Manifestation

Renowned known everywhere

According to Word

Holy of Holies

Enquire in His temple

Stay behind the vail

Behold great beauty

[12]Psalm twenty-seven and four

Seek after Kingdom

Where the real praises?

Shouting is not praising God

Dab on the devils head

Be on high alert

Stay posted no matter what

BANG – between the eyes

Took one Tylenol

Tired of being hand slapped

I'm not a pain freak

Hurt can't be voided

Surfaced from depth in despair

Looking for a hug

Sometimes love is pain

Chastisements and the rebukes

Endure good soldier

Bruised for all sinners

Opened not His mouth for us

Perfect LAMB, pure blood

Nobody like Christ

The one who suffered for us

Delivered and free

Rise above the past

Lean not to your own standing

God is the Father

Head held high, stand up

Value self, Woman of God

Be more than rubies

Lust and temptation

Generational curses

Set free and delivered

O LORD, hear my cry

Praying to get a breakthrough

He heard tears flowing

Loose me Succubus

Broke the bands of wickedness

No more chains, I'm free

I know who I am

Yes, more than a conqueror

I am He who's called

Every other line

Complaining about expense

Prodigal writer

O wasteful giver

Extravagant and reckless

Repentant spender

Knees buckling in

Palms dripping sweat, water sprout

No carpel tunnel

One, two, three, four, five

Every syllable numbered

There's humor in this

Mr. Prodigal

Inspiration, you gave me

Free of charge, thanks son.

Sunflower seeds crushed

Something dead to come alive

And grow among thorns

I thought about you

Not speaking to each other

What did I do wrong?

Pluck up from the roots

Spirit of disturbance

Slayed every demon

They didn't see me

God's perfect will and purpose

They only saw you

How interrupted,

His perfect will isn't ours

Prevent someone else

Social media

Weapon of Mass Distractions

Twitter and Facebook

Distracted my child

The winds blow, lighten flashing

He said, "[13]Peace Be Still"

Don't touch everything

Now, pretend to be a mime

Allow His will done

[14]Seek, and ye shall find

Call on the name of Jesus

Give Him what He's due

No works, faith is dead

Knock and the doors shall open

Financial harvest

Rent due on the 5th

God give seeds to the sowers

Learning to the trust God

[15]I AM the lender

No longer the borrower

That's word, speaking life

Armor Bearer walk

Guard your portals for Christ sake

Missionary style

Mark the perfect man

With having a servants heart

Willing to obey

Lowly in station

Having no authority

Meekness in spirit

Every morning

Repeating LOVE, PRAY, OBEY

Twenty-four hours

Yielding while walking

Remain steadfast in the word

Not my feet only

Submissive to Him

"Whatever you want, I'll do"

Answer the calling

Modest in manner

Obedient to the KING

And unimportant

Shaken together

[16]Saint Luke six and thirty-eight

Breast are bustin' loose

This my wealthy place

Decreeing and declaring love

I walk into it

Never suffer loss

Sowing seed is a lifestyle

God gives favor

WOE to the robber

Storehouse shall be filled with cheer

[17]Tithes and offerings

Now is harvest time

Rain moves toward the field

Reaping and sowing

Writing day and night

I in silence as He speaks

His thoughts are higher

Withdraw emotions

But what do they know about

The Christ whom I serve

Unpredictable

Praise report for His glory

Come through Holy Ghost

[18]Come on in the room,

He gives me my medicine

Jesus is healing

Stupid test results!

No manner of disease can,

Stay in the temple!

I believe the word,

[19]Isaiah fifty-three five

Yes, deliverance!

This process take time

I don't mind waiting on God

Make me like the moon

Bless your enemies

Pull it down in Jesus name

Bless the LORD with me

Face toward the ground

How treacherously afflicted

When he called my name

Keep us from evil

Direct our paths in the word

Stand up for our help

Fasting till noonday

Food seems to be everywhere

That's just the tempter

Fresh wind flowing breeze

Anointing fall down on me

Fill me once again

The Resurrection:

He died for us and rose again

Christ has all power

Disobedience

Tired of my own free will

Let's get back to God

Prophesy: Speak Life

[20]You shall live and not die

Speak over yourself

WOE! Out of my pain

Came beauty and strength from God

Troubles didn't last

Deeper and sincere

Wash me in the blood, Jesus

To another place

LORD, make me a house

Please, hold it down G.O.D.

Built upon a rock

Do without ceasing

And not quenching the spirit

Boldly before HIM

Somebody told me

About the pain afflicted

It was old man Job

We've cursed with our tongues

Blessings in the same manner

Once we were all Saul

The best way to get

Over pain is to talk about it openly

MINUTE

#Oppressed

Give back everything you stole

Hidden, you mole

Darkness, you wait

Hatred, you mate.

Contaminated all substance

Red eye, rubbin'

Strong hand, mischief

Murder witness.

The workers of iniquity,

No quality.

Secret demise,

Lies, can't hide.

Jesus Did It

It was cool receiving blessings

Ignored lessons

Active sinning

Death beginning

Praying through difficult smooth times

Stay sober mind

Take hold of faith

When finance break

Overcomer by Christ blood shed

Glory, not cred.

Resurrected,

Sin rejected.

Last Breath

[21]We know all things work together,

Stormy weather.

Natural beauty,

Whirl wind moody.

The dessert or wilderness,

Cursing or blessed.

Symbol of life,

Bridegroom and wife.

First winter, spring, summer, autumn

 Humor, gottem.

Youth or adult,

Breathing occult.

Divine Appointment

No one ask questions, why?

Assume a lie.

Covered up smiles,

Hit curve ball trails.

Meeting on purpose, the LORDS will,

Cost of yes, real.

No more hiding,

Who's presiding?

High off His word, who's offended?

Spread love, send it.

Perfect timing,

Mountain climbing.

Forgiven Slave

Held hostage at so many levels

Backwards pedal

Crying for help

Secrets I kept

Told Master, "I apologized,"

Uncircumcised.

Running away,

His word shall stay.

I will never be bound again,

Repent for sin.

Chains falling off,

Slow to wrath, boss!

Saints' Digest

Stay hungry for the word of God

Serve Christ, my job.

Keep me humble

Will not fumble.

Springing up a well of water

The KING's daughter

Anointing oil,

Sow in good soil.

Issue of blood doesn't exist

Denounce sickness

Eat this good food

Just like, you should

The Day After

Continue blessing God with pain

Blank vision stain

Three small letters

Carry better

Built up anger being a victim

Role-play, sitcom.

Un-forgiveness

Slap the hot piss,

Out of someone else different,

More time well spent.

Did you hear me?

Birthing dance feet.

A Minute with Jesus

If life is spent right, live for Christ!

He's the true knight.

Shining armor,

Now and later!

Christ been places we don't won' see,

Died on a tree.

Spit in the face,

Body, no trace.

Remember the times we were hurt?

Got mad, left church.

Love His goodness,

Return fullness.

Created Mess

In the beginning wasn't crap
His fingers snapped
Adam and Eve
Not Bob and Steve

Forbidden apple tasted sweet
And full of deceit
Sinners' purpose,
Received herpes.

Walking round naked unashamed
Guilty in pain.
Consuming WOE,
Forgiven? NO!

Cheat Codes

It's more than a testimony
It's not phony
Quick praise report
Keep it real short

Passing exams back to back
Scantrons marked black
Answers given
Never trippin'

Staying ready on high alert
Have faith with works
Who delivered?
Pulled the trigger.

Our Letter to Moses

You taught us well those forty years
With no seen fear
Led with a rod
Hidden in fog

We walked murmuring day and night
Spirit contrite
Heavens manna
No bananas

You didn't have to smite the stone
Promise, now gone.
No more roses,
Thank you Moses.

Purple Masquerade

I've learned to hide my sinful ways
Extra sweet, glazed.
Poker face strong.
Front, I put-on.

Quote Psalm one hundred verse seven
Preacher, Reverend,
Impersonate.
Holding dead weight.

Have love, peace, and prosperity,
Fancy party.
Dressing up sin,
Hatred within.

TANKA

This Ain't Deep

So as the LORD spoke to my inner fat person.

Them smoked ham hocks were calling my name,

I replied, "The belly is more than meat"

Controlla

I am hard to love.

Difficult to understand.

Rough round the edges.

LORD, soften every place,

That's been covered with concrete.

Clear Eyes

No day dreaming please

Keep rubbing until they tear

The vision, motto, and welcome.

Can you see it, even with no solution?

Not Today Satan

Spirit of distraction has to leave.

I will not be in bondage any longer.

Get yo stuff and go!

Eviction notice is served.

Tired of Sleeping

They say somebody got the key to unlock dreams.

Can't interpret, as it should be.

Somebody wake me up, I been dreaming.

Action and Works

Lord, as I repent

Saturate my spirit man.

God keep my heart pure.

I've never experienced

Freedom through faith like this God.

Shout out to Jesus

This relationship gets sweeter by the day.

New batch of mercies just to show he cares!

Been here since the womb.

I salute you, Christ!

More than Enough

More than a vision,

Words spoken daily aloud.

More than clapping hands,

Not just talking bout victory.

But living a lifestyle.

H2O

Aqua holder stands

Controversy all around

Hurt, harm or danger

Forget the rest, grab a can.

Die and go to burning hell

False Prophet

She preached with fire

Speaking loud and sparing not

Cut throat only way

They waved, got saved then forgave

Treatreusly delivered

Who tired of church?

The LORD getting His glory!

No more religion,

Whosoever will let come

Not nasty but transparent

Your name above all

Manifest in me, Jesus

Let your will be done

Daily sun up to sun down

LORD, I'm chasing after you

Brim, running over

If you provide the fire

Here is my body

My reasonable service

Accept your servant again

Woman, thou art loosed

Whom the son sets free, is free

Indeed, nothing more

Deny thyself everyday

Pick up your cross, follow Him

With the ghost, I'm filled

Hearing everything to me

LORD, teach me thy ways

Consuming fire, destroy

Yes, Master I'll obey you

Holy Ghost, fill me up

I'm naked & not ashamed

I present my heart

Reveal all the dark secrets

Clothe me Jesus with your love

No light shines through eye

Tainted soul no one can help

Bruh, God gone check you

Stop using your power wrong

But Christ will do the increase

The background lover

Don't fall asleep while tested

Transfer happening

Gave up as though your presence

Never existed this life time

FREE VERSE

Life's Rehearsal

We moved to the beat of our actions, no dance rehearsal. In a state of denial, who can replace us? Who can move like us?

Systematically he led, as I followed, no blue bird. Keep scrolling across the path of un-forgiveness and still in motion, mud whole. We move, we groove, we should, and we could although we won't, not by choice but by force.

I tried to keep up, he gave me an "E" for effort, we still moved together, one less than the other. The two aren't half, both are whole, together or separate, we move. Travelling the road of honesty, we left our song behind.

Who's bad? The emotions, feelings, actions not taking hold to us as we shook and jive.

Grab my hand in the motion of sickness and tired, tired of me, tired of not being faithful to he.

Who's moved? Who's left? Who separated us?

We still on the move, right now we're together hoping for a new experience.

That Late Text

I wanted to write you this long ten line multimedia text, but no.

It would've had nothing to do with us. I've seen the way other girls look at you and I totally am ignored, as a shadow from someone else.

Speak to us, without the fuss.

Don't get mad, don't cuss.

Stop passing me while I speak to everyone else. Yes, I'm an open book, you put back on the shelf. I'm still thinking about sending a lengthy text while your number blocked.

Is that why we don't speak?

Should I be in shock?

We laugh along when we hear joke, the visible sin as they wonder and poke. Help me understand one thing right now; would you still play blind if I was with child?

November 12th 2016

Give me everything you think is yours. Not materialistic, but the physical, your spiritual and the intellectual, I want it all says the LORD.

They make a mockery because of your philosophy but the sick always yelling "doctor please".

What now? What more could yall need?

Fed you manna with some water, gave a harvest when no one sowed seeds. All I've been doing is handing out incentives, maybe if I spared yall life, sooner than later for me you'll live. Still no regret when you forgot about me, remember the time they said you lost your mind? How they lied on your actions, sleeping on me, no city mattress.

Wake up, my child or the end is near, you will soon want help all I want is "yes" is the first step.

November 13th 2016

Watching TV there came a revelation, the reason for downfalls there's no declaration.

The mind becomes idol with no concentration continual being tempted and having a thing for temptation.

In quiet time presenting God a proclamation, if the spirit is full that's the demonstration.

99 won't get it, 100% sanctification.

Waiting for New Jerusalem, is the destination.

From a babe in Christ, to living a holy life, sounds like graduation.

The temple finds rest, which is our savior habitation.

Thank God for another experience another visitation, another day in your will for complete manifestation.

November 19th 2016

I was created to praise and was taught to write, made to love but would start a fight. I knew how to rap, the lyrics I wrote. Still can't swim and barely staying afloat. Quick to Google search exactly what I need, when it comes to God, all I do is stay begging and plead.

Created to serve, anointed to give.

No more destroying, I'm ready to build. Kingdom minded (agent) on duty for post, crying when rebuked but laugh at a roast. I can't understand when God says, "trust" wanted to give up salvation to follow lust. These were times I wasn't myself, like a rag doll being played then put back on the shelf. Ashes to ashes my words became dust, when the rain came, my bones began to rust. Overflow of iniquity so I started to drown…

HELP ME PLEASE!

But no one heard the sound in the middle of a forest, falling like a tree, practicing to preach but all they heard was me.

A New Level

I searched so many places to see where you were and almost

Every time there was no you, The one I searched for, the one I longed for, the one I am in need of

I couldn't find you there, the place I stayed, the place I laid, the place I played

Until you moved me, took me, woke me up and shook me,

Now you have me here, Somewhere new, somewhere unknown, somewhere close to home,

I'm welcomed here, stationed here, prepared here and tested here,

Thank you for moving me and showing me not just telling me but teaching me.

Thank you for your spirit, Jesus!

February 11th 2017

Have your way in me Jesus so your glory can be revealed. Rise up demon slayers that is out to kill, and tear down Satan's kingdom brick upon brick, saints of God shall be in health and denounce every sickness, Every manner of evil which is to attack, LORD cover your people, stress free generations we going back to back! To Edom without forbidden fruits, pluck up the spirit of homosexuality starting from the root. Being entangled with some mess not even the Apostle could pray Cause in lust seemed so right, flesh too weak, couldn't even fight, to save a life, to denounce strife, stay away from that man's wife. OH can somebody just pray much harder, forget about politically correct, the question posed;

"Who is the Father?"

"Who do we serve?"

"Where is our home?"

"Is our light shining daily or are our intentions wrong?"

"Did yall hear me sing when we all song?"

I asked God to have mercy on my soul, heal me Jesus from the crown of my head to the pinky toes, both feet and not my feet alone, but my hands and my head. Who's made their bed in the pits of hell

To know the LORD never left just like an unused toy, I was put back on the shelf, life took it's course throwing blow after blow. Late night show hashtag "Aww Hell Snow", when I flash back I begin to laugh. Thanking Christ for this journey, this path, this moment to commune with the Father, I bless God for accepting me as his daughter.

They Counted Me... Out!

Yall did more than that; yall put me in, what's wrong with my last name?

Why you still say, "Jen"? Help me to understand because it is me who's misunderstood every time yall gossip, God said, "Do good". Do you think I really sowed into you? That seed was on assignment and your colors showed too! It's fine and I'm cool if you don't do me, I'm still your sister, now what say ye? Start to question my own actions, "Do I really respect yall or am I trying to please the Pastor"?

Heard yall say, "I think I'm better than the multitude" so yall can read thoughts? They counted me out cause I have visible faults. Check yourself before you make someone else feel worthless and ashamed, I can speak life or play mind games.

See I've learned when people doubt me that is the time to go harder, don't be shocked when I become a starter. The first shall be last and the last shall be first, "do my prophet no harm" or the latter shall be worse.

About the Author

Jennifer Lorraine Alexander, found her love for poetry in middle school, she then began to write short stories as well.

Jennifer was born and raised in Belle Glade, Florida where she is enjoys Saturday mornings at the library reading and using the computers for her advancement in writing and other social media activities.

Ms. Alexander is currently an employee of the School District of Palm Beach County working with special needs children as a bus attendant.

Jennifer didn't take her writing serious until reaching sophomore year in college. Her literature professor pushed her thinking creativity to the next level.

The author's social media platforms

Twitter: @Googlefoundme

Instagram: @WritingsfromJenn

Youtube: Mc08Nugget

END NOTES

---

[1] **1 Corinthians 8:1 (KJV)**
Now as touching things offered unto idols, we know that we all have knowledge. Knowledge puffeth up, but charity edifieth.

[2] **Isaiah 12:2 (KJV)**
Behold, God is my salvation; I will trust, and not be afraid: for the LORD JEHOVAH is my strength and my song; he also is become my salvation.

[3] **Luke 9:23 (KJV)**
And he said to them all, If any man will come after me, let him deny himself, and take up his cross daily, and follow me.

[4] **Matthew 22:14 (KJV)**
For many are called, but few are chosen.

[5] **Psalm 91:2 (KJV)**
I will say of the LORD, He is my refuge and my fortress: my God; in him will I trust.

[6] **1 Thessalonians 5:17 (KJV)**
Pray without ceasing.

[7] **Isaiah 54:17 (KJV)**
No weapon that is formed against thee shall prosper; and every tongue that shall rise against thee in judgment thou shalt condemn. This is the heritage of the servants of the LORD, and their righteousness is of me, saith the LORD.

[8] **Hebrews 11:1 (KJV)**
Now faith is the substance of things hoped for, the evidence of things not seen.

[9] **Luke 7:50 (KJV)**
And he said to the woman, Thy faith hath saved thee; go in peace.

[10] **Psalm 51:7 (KJV)**
Purge me with hyssop, and I shall be clean: wash me, and I shall be whiter than snow.

[11] **3 John 1:2 (KJV)**
Beloved, I wish above all things that thou mayest prosper and be in health, even as thy soul prospereth.

Psalm 27:4 (KJV)

One thing have I desired of the LORD, that will I seek after; that I may dwell in the house of the LORD all the days of my life, to behold the beauty of the LORD, and to enquire in his temple.

Mark 4:39 (KJV)

And he arose, and rebuked the wind, and said unto the sea, Peace, be still. And the wind ceased, and there was a great calm.

Matthew 7:7 (KJV)

Ask, and it shall be given you; seek, and ye shall find; knock, and it shall be opened unto you:

Deuteronomy 28:12 (KJV)

The LORD shall open unto thee his good treasure, the heaven to give the rain unto thy land in his season, and to bless all the work of thine hand: and thou shalt lend unto many nations, and thou shalt not borrow.

Luke 6:38 (KJV)

Give, and it shall be given unto you; good measure, pressed down, and shaken together, and running over, shall men give into your bosom. For with the same measure that ye mete withal it shall be measured to you again.

Malachi 3:10 (KJV)

Bring ye all the tithes into the storehouse, that there may be meat in mine house, and prove me now herewith, saith the LORD of hosts, if I will not open you the windows of heaven, and pour you out a blessing, that there shall not be room enough to receive it.

Georgia Mass Choir » Come On In The Room

Isaiah 53:5 (KJV)

But he was wounded for our transgressions, he was bruised for our iniquities: the chastisement of our peace was upon him; and with his stripes we are healed.

Psalm 118:17 (KJV)

I shall not die, but live, and declare the works of the Lord.

Romans 8:28 (KJV)

And we know that all things work together for good to them that love God, to them who are the called according to his purpose.

Made in the USA
Columbia, SC
16 July 2018